Sleeping with the Moon

Sleeping with the Moon

Poems by
Colleen J. McElroy

University of Illinois Press

Urbana and Chicago

Library of Congress Cataloging-in-Publication Data
McElroy, Colleen J.
Sleeping with the moon : poems /
by Colleen J. McElroy.
p.   cm.
ISBN 978-0-252-03235-6 (alk. paper)
ISBN 978-0-252-07476-9 (pbk. : alk. paper)
I. Title.
PS3563.A2925S57   2007
811'.54—dc22   2007016985

Other books by Colleen J. McElroy

POETRY

Music From Home: Selected Poems
Winters Without Snow
Lie and Say You Love Me
Queen of the Ebony Isles
Bone Flames
What Madness Brought Me Here
Travelling Music

FICTION

Jesus and Fat Tuesday
Driving Under the Cardboard Pines

NON-FICTION

Speech and Language Development of the Preschool Child
A Long Way From St. Louie (travel memoirs)
Over the Lip of the World: Among the Storytellers of Madagascar
Page to Page: Retrospectives of Writers from the *Seattle Review*
   (anthology)

Acknowledgments

Thanks to the editors and publishers of the following journals in which these poems first appeared, some in slightly different versions: "The Company She Keeps," *Age Ain't Nothing But a Number: Black Women Explore Midlife;* "The Year I Found Myself Under Two Blue Moons," *Massachusetts Review;* "Light Reflecting Glass in the Evelyn Room," *Manhattan Review;* "Mother Love," *ZYZZYVA;* "Mae West Chats It Up with Bessie Smith," *Crab Orchard Review* and *Blues Poems* (Kevin Young, ed., Penguin, 2003); "What Happened to the Rabbit," *Big Muddy;* "The Vixen Speaks to the Last Full Moon of the Century," *Hayden's Ferry;* "Some Are Dead and Some Are Living," *Black Scholar;* "First Date After Fifty," *Eyeball;* "Electra" and "Catching Gar," *Arkansas Review;* "You and Me and Veronica Lake," *Manhattan Review;* "Pillow Book," *New Letters;* "Bad Slam Broadway," "Moon Over Marakesh," and "Eartha Kitt Takes the Old Woman Shopping for Red Shoes," *Obsidian III;* "Boys Will Be" and "Fairy Tales," *Cranky;* "Frostbite," *African American Review;* "In Praise of Older Women," "Drawing a Line in the Sand," *Nimrod;* "Teaching G.I.s to Dance," *Haight Ashbury Literary Journal;* "Unlearning the Brothers Grimm," *Nocturnes;* "Moon Over Turtle Island," *Seattle Woman;* "Ballad for the Blue Moon Tavern," *Long Journey: Contemporary Northwest Poets* (David Biespiel, editor); "Some Are Dead and Some Are Living," *Black Scholar;* and *The Ringing Ear: Black Poets Lean South,* A Cave Canem Anthology (Nikki Finney, editor).

My thanks to David Lehman for accepting "Mae West Chats It Up with Bessie Smith" for *Best American Poetry 2001* (New York: Schribner, 2001).

Some I loved who are dead
were watchers of the moon
    and knew its lore:
    planted seeds,
trimmed their hair,

    Pierced their ears
for gold hoop earrings
    as the moon advised.

—ROBERT HAYDEN

Contents

PART I

" . . . left with nothing but the moon to hold onto."

Pillow Book

(for Denise Levertov)

in the absence of a lover
books occupy my bed's extra pillow
those words have never failed me
though paper ages—grows brittle
every phrase stays muscular
laughing at all the right places
saddened by slights by deaths
the significance of even simple
language: curtains blowing at a window
a cup abandoned on a table
    I hear them breathing Denise confesses
    more surely than ever any man beside me
    she tells me how on her pillow books
    take hold of her dreams: a sort of
    Levertov then and now she says
    age so deceptive the difference between
    50–60 becomes more like 20–40
    time faster than any clock

    Lady Nagiko writes in her pillow book:

        the mirror grown cloudy the lover
        on his second nighttime visit the scent
        of incense burning: things not to forget

nights my bed is occupied solely by books
and lingering smells of some lover's sweat
so vague time has fallen away: leaves
a dim profile—a name on the tip of my tongue—
I remember riding my bike in a park Denise says
in London and the war just beginning I think
there was a wrought iron fence benches

a few pigeons I remember leaves curling brown
I never learned to drive a car even later
    after there were men to do that for me—
    we abandon our tea cups for memory
    offering up a wordless page or two of youth
    as do those lovers returning in dreams
    resting their heads on the cup of my pillow
    exchanging stories as if one has spoken
    to another and all of them heavy with sighs

> *the Empress wore a robe of green*
> *Chinese silk beneath an unlined*
> *jacket a skirt of elephant silk*
> *nothing could compare to her beauty*

the shape of your pillow holds old lovers
the way an elbow rests in a palm
the way his voice sounds each morning
just as you awaken from a dream
where in the dead of night you rise
thinking: he's gone — later it comes true
this dream for years you've resisted
you lift up on one elbow and stare
at his face etching all the lines
into your memory an effort to keep him close
    you will remember only the small things
    Denise says: the way you quarreled
    one holiday when the roast burned
    the pepper too coarsely ground on Sundays
    Monday morning's after party face
    the face we are born with and one
    we grow into and one that we earn
    the body records a life dutifully
    without specific instructions or directions
    long forgotten words in creases and folds
    no day separate from the other and easy

to read as any book from front to back
or reverse except in half sleep
where you retell the story to suit

    where is a book before it is born
    is one book born inside another
    how old does a book have to be
    before it can give birth

I am the lover of books my life gives
in my youth I learned to love words
how they felt on the shape of my tongue
I practiced languages I wanted to know
the gestures honed in a mirror
fingers tracing the angle of a jaw
sweet hair curled at the nape of the neck
    don't confuse writing of love and finding it
    Denise warns and I tell her how in dreams
    profiles blend one into another
    until lovers blur with each take
    how strange that most of love
    I say lives in the imagination

    books and lovers Nagiko writes:
    I have had the good
    fortune to enjoy them equally

let's say it started in June
when no one kept an appointment
and commitments were swept out
the door with the last of spring
cleaning—or let's say Denise tells me
it was in the kitchen at a party you noticed
how familiar the little gesture passing
between them not what they said but in the eyes
    silence I tell her was a family emblem
    at five in St. Louis during the war

I'd sneak into my mother's room watch
her sleeping behind a curtain of dreams
her eyes moving under lids as if she
and all black women were reading books
of their men off fighting for a country
willing to forget them for the color
of dark skin—those days passed slowly
years five to six moving at snail's pace
the world blowing up in bits and pieces
I thought I'd never grow up whole and
dreams would come true if only I crossed
my fingers and said: I wish on the moon
and pain was easily erased—now I know
Everything that happens is to be adored

    in her pillow book Lady Nagiko writes:

        understand the hand cannot write itself
        closed eyes cannot read

in the garden patio Denise sets three cups
on the table—curtains billow at the window
time compressed stopped for a moment
I have brought a lover who makes
casual conversation and I think:
If only we had made love
only to each other when we made love
    sweet dreams Denise says as we leave
    where has the time gone when yesterday
    so close seems years away—the cups
    left on the garden table something
    from a dream and each time I clear
    the pillow of books beside me
    a lover's breath at night seems shallow
I have become *la femme d'un certain âge*
falling into the cup of dreams where innocent
breezes pose no warnings and there is nothing

between me and the night but curtains moving
before an open window—books and lovers
on the pillow beside me both breathing
deep their own dreams—a place
where sweet desire never leaves

Mother Love

five floors above the ground
my only view the park
peaceful the shrink says
a place to think
I am waiting to talk

about my absent daughter
the park is deserted
only a figure in the center
changing clothes inside
a sleeping bag the grass

around him evenly green
my daughter once again
has changed her mind
about being my daughter
I am puzzled why

is the park so empty
except for the quick change
artist centered on the slope
of grass flushed green
why does he prefer

all that space public
for such a private act
my daughter never modest
has cloaked herself in Jesus
proclaiming Him in public

loud as the doors she once
slammed almost covering how
beautiful she has grown since
that first time she shed home
at 18 declaring herself a woman

the man struggles like Houdini
changing pants shirt shoes
dead center the park
privacy the shrink says
is sometimes dangerous

out in the open no one
can surprise you with sudden
moves my daughter has moved
two continents an ocean away
somewhere she sleeps holding

tight to her beliefs
nothing else will do
none of my unused acts
of contrition supplications
I forgot almost before I left

the confessional booth
none of grandma's hymns
or my mother's warnings
I am alone under an empty sky
staring at a man in the park

his task done he stows
belongings in a bed roll
leaving a small impression grass
bent a fracture barely visible
seemingly warm to my naked eye

Catching Gar

we build a fire—a false moon
to lure them toward the light::
catching gar my father says

is a matter of timing
they're all teeth he says
uglier than any mud fence

and full of piss flesh
he baits a hook for what
we'll eat :: jack salmon

sweet fleshed as spring
he loads my bait—the .22::
tells me how he fished

in Georgia—fat channel cats
caught on a shoestring
while white folks slept::

the Mississippi rolls by
under a pork bellied moon
the brightest light our fire

bait for gar swimming up
from river bottom—needle-
nosed and long as rusted saws::

my father clicks shut the .22
tells me to aim with both
eyes open :: in the car

my mother sleeps open-mouthed
nothing will wake her
not the pop-pop of the wicked

.22 I load and reload—not
the flop of fish tossed
bony head toward tail in clean

shots—not the flutter of night
birds or random owl warnings::
this story is ours—father

to daughter—this fine art
of killing that marks
him a soldier :: the odds

of any battle—death in sight
and only the moon to light the way

I Speak to the Girl Some Dim Boy Loves

(after Hugo)

It takes the table girl a week to learn the route:
The patient spray of table tops, the swirl of cloth
The food to scrap and dishes on the belt become
Her world—students at their complicated books

Are of another life—but in six months
A year or less, she'll have their manners down:
A little splash of color to her polyester dress
A flick of wrist or hair, a lipstick smear and
She'll be more like one of them than any of them dares.

This is the state solution—employing her kind
Here among the population who decides
The number of any kind a society can abide.
We are the learned few, the two or three

Who make the rules, who read the books
That tell us how humane we've made this life:
The charity of how we grow polite enough
To pin the handicapped to our routines.

The table girl keeps thirty tables clean
And speaks only to the boy who works the dishes
From conveyer belt to sink, who elevates and leaves
Her hopeful as her dyed blonde hair.

But her face will not grow beyond its flat despair
And I believe I've fathomed all of this alone as dishes
Slip across the belt's rubber sheet, until one day
I place humanity beside my Goodwill stare and ask:

How goes your day? She says: "Monday, Clive dropped
The baby on its head—things ain't been the same since.
Birds seem louder—the stream is down to a trickle.
I 'spect we'll bury the baby tomorrow." My cup falls over.
She clatter-bangs more dishes on the belt.

Anniversary

before the night is over
he will fold her like a letter
heels over head over knees
into shoulders his idea
he says of what makes
her tick in a decade he forgets
what he has spent
so much for one
body part so little
for the heart a gameboy
bartering life the carpal
pull of every slap-bang brings
a little kiss alternating
Sisterwoman and Zap Mama
Angel Baby Madonna
battered and curled
like an old fetus his
Sugahgirl his Honeybunch
his Little Woman celebrated
in paper, wood, silver & gold

Most Wanted

what I remember most
not passion
but simple desire
how once while we were
on an errand I watched
an arrest a nice couple
both middle-aged
ordinary perhaps running
an errand (like us?)
and lit by a backstreet moon
the woman neither pretty
nor plain and her man
handsome in his way
standing so certain
in handcuffs and she
in tears her face caught
in an escapade gone sour
a bust and how the cops
allowed for one moment
a last kiss that you
beside me never noticed
and later said you didn't
remember the couple
or how in that peculiar
light they resembled us

Sleeping with the Moon

homelessness: to be uprooted, to be without shelter or provisions;
    RARE: affording no home

months after you left home, someone saw you on the bus, so quiet you
sat, peaceful they said behind your horn-rimmed glasses, black against the
blackness of your skin burnt from the dust of nightmares, peaceful they
said and barefoot though the weather was not yet warm not cold, one
morning someone saw you near the park walking past the statue of the
city's great pioneers the founders of wide streets and homes fit for grand
families while the rain fell in great swoops over and over and we dared to
call it spring behind the safety of plate glass windows, wind blowing gauze
white curtains roses and poppies in gleaming china vases — they said they
knew you by your closely-cut hair, trusting eyes large behind oval black
rimmed glasses your face grown dry mouthed and wary, the easy laughter
burning inside what's left of your dreams after another night of sleeping
rough with no house but the moon — someone said they saw you on the
ferry heading west beyond the San Juans beyond the thirty mile limit, it
must have been you they said the look so familiar they almost called you
by name, I know you would not have answered I know I barely knew
you myself glimpsed on the corner after the coldest night the weather
offered, I knew you only by the tilt of your head the thin curtain of tears you
kept from falling on your cheeks and I pulled to the curb and wept—don't
worry you said this is my demon—and I wept for all the demons that haunt
us and the little boy who trusted too easily, laughter your only addiction,
and the way my arms ached to pull in the body trembling under that ragged
sleeping bag, to rock you once more to read a favorite story and hold back
the raw scrap of time as the world rushed into another day and I curled
into myself and I wept

Codex: Frostbite

the cold took the life
out of him left him
stumbling into spring

the cold took the life
he might have had left
and left his hands like base-

ball mitts feet toeless
inside the charity of new
sneakers stumbling duck-

footed out of the cold
that took from him the last
scrap of laughter the fool-

hearty *joie de vivre*
that once kept him
alive cold or not

the cold singed toes
turned them into root bulbs
fingers into overripe plums

the cold took beauty
and left instead bitter
hope the dream at last

floating inside the sleep
of waking the drugged sleep
that wouldn't notice the cold

floating in the waiting dark
the sleep that overtakes
cold and leaves him

stumbling alone beautiful
barefoot boy the black man stolen
in a *danse macabre*

snapping clean against the cold
hard bed of streets the un-
bending rule to keep

such cold away from decent
folks such fear in trembling
bones such alone alone alone

without a home to speak of
without a wife to tuck the sheets
or child to put the kettle on

to keep the cold away away
where it cracks like an eggshell
a blue streak in the thin

ice of bruising a break a burn
of cold the insult of loss
at night in the dimness of door-

ways where business has ended
and everyone no one sees what
lies there in that bundle of rags

someone's brother someone's child
where the wind whips debris into air
thin as a river waiting under the ice

Codex: Diagnosis

the shadows between bones
shrink smaller than slivers
of moon or splinters of wood

doctors say you look
like a poster child for bones
bent on breaking like stones

strangers say you look
like yourself today and you
think : : if not me who?

you feel bones splinter
and one day after you wouldn't
look in the mirror you look

no longer like yourself—bones
turn to powder, joints to wood
one day when you seem to look

unlike yourself, others look
away, mistake you for a wounded
doe, an accident someone slipped

up and left breathing—wouldn't
keep or throw away—friends too
polite to say you look

like death warmed over and you look
at a hole in the sky, wonder who
unplugged what's leaking from bones

gone to seed and splinters
from water that won't freeze and one
of those days everything slips

out of focus and you look
at the dinner plate as if you've
never seen food, fingers all bones

sinking into themselves—you
bent to cycle in and out of pain one
day at a time, thinking who

would have believed this would
have become me and one day
decide this :: one day you'll
look like yourself and no other

Drawing a Line in the Sand

on chemo the brain
    flickers like a strobe . . .
follows a bouncing ball
    traveling along a song nobody

knows . . . you are always
    tired learning to sing
the song chemo demands . . .
    the brain restless zig . . .

zags in mental tachycardia . . .
    grows tired until zapped
onto the next stop . . . someone
    has salted your waterglass

everything smells of mildew
    and all you know is out
of synch . . . you nap for the 3rd
    time in 1 day and 5 minutes

later you are tired of propping
    open your eyelids . . . 3–5–6–8
how do you hallucinate . . .
    grey zone some subway terminal

where all trains switch tracks
    at a moment's notice . . . switch
back out of reason's reach . . .
    no wonder your hair falls out . . .

no wonder you can't recall
if you pulled it by the roots
    you can't remember your roots
or what you'd give for a plate

    of fried food and sweet pudding . . .
you're tired of being careful
    tired of trying to remember
yesterday or five minutes ago . . .

    or how much hair you've lost
and what gets caught between
    the skitter scatter of what
passes for thought and what

    you tell the doctor who looks
younger than your daughter . . .
    not that it matters when
the lights go out . . . and at last

    you sink into sweet fatigue . . .
the doctor changes the dosage . . .
    drawing a line in the sand
and hoping it will stick . . .

    you let memory take you
on the liquid highway past do not
    enter past aimless circles
the fine art of doing nothing

    in a land of random thoughts . . .
someone's left a pot on the stove
    you smell it burning . . . now your head
is full of notes you'll never get to mail

Chilblains

you have taken woolens out of storage
fixed the furnace waved
goodbye to the last of the geese
trailing lazy V's across a rosy
Cascade sky you are relearning
the grammar of insulation
the punctuation of antifreeze and subtle
changes in Arctic seasons you're gearing
up for the big one fraught with memories
of drifts tall as houses off Kansas
and Nebraska plains by five o'clock
nightbirds call . . . *hiver* . . . *hiver* under
a thin slice of moon while the sun
loses its shadow you've read all the signs
you know what's coming your feet begin
yearning for the covering of fur
or the small of a lover's back temperatures
drop as you replay the phrase: "Colder than
a witch's tit" without malice toward gender
your heart's not in it you want heat—light—
anything that turns into laughter

Blues for Spring

it should happen
on a train a face
you see in passing

a glance a kiss
just for the asking
it should happen

in a room where tea
is served in thin china
cups and Mendelssohn

or Brahms musical verse
sugars the air
or perhaps it happens

in a bar where Dexter
Gordon and his crowd
of hoarse laughter

wail the mighty sax
and your friend Gordon
calls suddenly

from Costa Rica
out-of-the-blue and says
do you remember? and you

recognize only the steel
blue of the northern sky
forlorn as winter

or a note welded thin
to sorrow the horizon
so clear so close

so naked a love
that should come
should happen soon

In Praise of Older Women

once when a blue finger of moonlight fell
through the window she happened upon
a neighbor asleep in the space of slats
the blinds all but obscuring the sight of him
slumbering under the moon—cock and balls
languishing ripe as fruit against his thigh
hanging in such innocence unsheathed she almost
called out fool that she was: Beware: such delicate
sights have driven more than one woman to despair
instead she watched him breathe—relishing
for a moment that secret space where night
grows soft and the moon's detumescence forgives—
and where if this jeweled light holds they might
strip themselves of years if only for one night

PART II

the moon trapped in the window of the sex shop
defines the pleasures of Ben-Wa

You and Me and Veronica Lake

I used to smoke before they opened
my chest and surgery filled the dark
clouds roiling and rain turned acid.
My best friend died lungs full of ashes
her hula skirts dry grass rustling
in the corner then another
friend and poems scattered on pages
like incomplete love letters
sprinkles from old pipes.
I used to smoke after lost loves

and Johnny-come-lately's
smoke rings signalling the best
sex or the worst the room
clouded blue under a moon gone bad
tobacco sweat leather apple smell
into sunrise stink of an old shoe.
I used to hold up my finger to find
the moon the end stained yellow
smoke rings dancing above my head
like haloes of broken moons.
I smoked past several husbands

and loyal friends lungs charred
black and sliced on a surgeon's plate
from the burning kiss and coffin nails
voice lost in phlegm blooming cloudy
white to yellow. I smoked afternoons
thinking I think I believe smoking
makes anything possible the sexiest
come-hither look or wise pause

taking you straight to the stroke
of the pen. I smoked with silver
holsters the best tobaccos coughs

levelling the field. I smoked
with gangsters and preachers
and mothers waiting for diapers
and fitted sheets oh we were
the best in those days when
the best could be measured easily
by filters and name brands and what's
up front that counts. I smoked
when glory days were good days
and mystery was repartee in a bar
snappy lines thrown by some old

Viceroy leading man to the nearest
femme fatale. I smoked happily
gloriously helter-skelter
and pell-mell. I smoked when suzy
parker was The Face dionne
warwick crooned for bacharach and cadillacs
had fins. I smoked to live
fast love hard die young and rise
again like a fresh face from celluloid
heaven waiting beside a smoky piano
spotlight a blurred moon behind blue clouds
and me singing torch songs forever.

First Date after Fifty

all nerves and questions
about what it takes to cut
the mustard or make the grade
long after you've taken
extension courses in lonely
you try on smiles like a corsage
or old dancing shoes stored
away since high school and
everyone you know is younger
than yesterday you remember
spending three months in Virginia
looking at the weather channel
your own heart cast inside a storm
now only you can figure out what's
wet and what's not you're stuck
say: this time I know more
and out the door with no one guessing
Salome had seven veils
you've kept the eighth

The Company She Keeps

finally she no longer
worries about the moon
and children about
the socks missing
in the wash or the mail
that arrives late
now she refuses to cover
her lust justly seeks
the most prodigious
outlet the lover
immune to age who parlays
time into skill
oh she's practiced
running down the beach
into the sea without
worry of drowning
or being pulled
in by undertow
and she's good
at what she does

she no longer cares
if neighbors catch
her in the act
yelling like a banshee
over each conquest
caught in the blaze
of a fire she makes
every night where
she is the flint
he the match she lights

she shocks slim hipped
youth who believe they
own all that is delicious
this *flagrante delicto*
this one act she coddles
to perfection
I'm warning you she says:

let me in the door and
I'll take the room let
me in the room and
I'll claim the house let
me in the house and
I'll own the block let
me onto the street and
the town is mine so
best move now cause
I'm landlady here
and you're never
too old to learn

he leans over
dismisses the pain
in his old joints
kisses her toes

Love Letters

for days I wait
for the Fed Ex truck

how do we communicate
what the fuck

email fax semaphore smoke
a sign that says:

watch this site for changes
a robin in the window box

a crow calling from the wire
condos of flirted doorways

I'd meet you in some dark
alley take your pick

let's be grown-ups
kiss while it's still hot

Boys Will Be

I no longer admire men
for just being them
selves if boys will be

let them be adults
grown into flat
stomachs and a head

full of hair let them
ask before they take
and pass on bad jokes

let me have patience
Lord to stroll past
long thighs and hard

muscle let me see
in that chest of springy hair
something animal getting out

and the smell of box elders
after a spring rain
let me know men don't change

fast only superman does
and he needs a phone booth
let me find a lover

who makes love like a tenor
and when he hits the high notes
the whole damn world stops dead
in its tracks to listen

Lust

what I remember: the hotel
and someone fucking in the next room

making love, you said, as if
words raised the grunts and groans

into a romantic interlude—that night
we made love—sweat seeped

through the periwinkle walls, the sheets
held our bodies close, grunts turned

into murmurs and the moon rose
bright as a new quarter in the flattened

sky—the next morning I waited
in the lobby dressed up
and no place to go

Blinded by the Moon

the miracle is not the moon
grown full in a night black sky
or even the stars visible
in the window above your shoulders
constellations pulsing in your neck
but how my fingers awakened
with only the moon to guide the way

the miracle is not how the moon
navigates through islands of stars
but how the imprint of my fingers
on your arm lines up like the path
of stars and how in the dark
I see where every movement
means merely I am holding on

my love we are here where
earth turns on its axis
and the moon trapped in a triangular
window is reflected again in a mirror
a double sided moon a triple moon
four shadowing the first
all caught in crepuscular light
Saturn dozing underneath

how could we see in the dark
with that old razzle dazzle flush
in the window hiding
the bruise of fingers of elbows
and knees the old moon dance
of Druids and Ibos
how did we hold the memory
of days full of broad light

but oh moon I have learned
to wash my hands in this thy dish
that love has brought to me

Remarks Beneath the Visiting Moon

tell me how you get here I say
I want the map to keep in my head
tell me when do you turn inland
off the highway and what
houses what lights lead the way
tell me how you remember and what
lets you navigate I want
to be with you when the road
curves bends and dances
in the rearview mirror
tell me if my smell taste
lingers on your mouth hands
tell me how I fall into
the shape of your words
your breath beside me
on the pillow tell me how
in the dark I can write
your name shamelessly on every
window tell me how
I can assume the shape of your
body holding me tell me I say
I am hopelessly helplessly
in love at 60 still going on 16
and no sunset moonrise will
ever be the same

Tango Moon

can I touch you yes and maybe no not here but there
    watch moonlight moonshaft moonbath
tumble spill and reappear in folds and creases
smells and molds and morning dew
    will you trust me after midnight lover
kiss me listen here::

    someone's walking near the window there a shadow
in the moonlight hush . . . I'm here just hold me

    tell me now why you chose me here's a word
for I adore you and another not as empty
falling in the cup of ears
    how I love it when you touch me kiss me
    tickle squirm and hold me here tighter::

one last sigh while I slip onto this altar
    under lunar light this love

caress my shoulders hips and fingers your tongue
it makes me shiver swoon and moan oh my dearest
    darling mine this room has grown so hot
take off your shirt and look my love my sweet
    oh the sky is full of moon

Heartbreak Moon on the Strait of Juan de Fuca

the night I fell in love
with the moon—the bay
spread out so clear fish leapt
into the space between light
and water—the moon was my only
choice—a gift like the sprig
of blue spruce and pine cones
I once received with a note:
come home my love come home

the night so clear I fell
into the mirror of water
pulling in the moon slice
by slice until only love
mattered and sweet water
teasing light from the sky
in moon streaks blue—
I watched my fingers stir
the ripples and plankton burst
in flashes of luminescence

giving off light without heat:
a lunar dance reflected
in phosphorescent trails—
the tails of fish or comets
fallen from the sky—fingertips
leaving streaks of light like
the kiss of fire electric
or some brief caress vanishing
too quickly in what little
touching we did in too few days—

that night you turned my head
until I was left with only
the moon to kiss me—
I would have preferred
you but the moon beckoned
floating incandescent
a glass marble drifting
in the dark pool of night sky—
I held my breath and wished

to stay forever earthbound where
pine trees whispered to wind
and water caught in the play
of light—lost I said I'm lost
to love and I can tell you now
the moon laughed—poor dog
it said, poor rabbit coming back
for one more try

In the Blind Eye of Love's Shiny Moon

The road was a ribbon of moonlight over the purple moors
When the highwayman came riding . . . up to the old inn door
—ALFRED NOYES, *THE HIGHWAYMAN*

There is a madman at my door,
A gentle man who baits me with sweet flower
Words that bloom like bruises and last for hours.
A man who asks for little but my heart
Who touches me in pieces with apologies
For his stabs at love which he says
Were honed on another woman's sharp edges, and I
Believe the anger that fills his eyes with fear.

There is a soft kiss at my door
And words that soothe with innocence
My pain of losing once again
This house of thin composure
Where I expose the keloids of my failures.
This madman knows too well what my love
Needs and waits to see me turn
Into what he believes all women yearn
To be—a moon struck beast to strip
The coolness of his skin.

There is a madman at my door
Who speaks to me in anecdotes of by-gone
Sins, the ageless ghosts and friends
Almost forgotten except for his half-truths
Banked against a blameless mother's promise.
But none of us are off the hook in this
Insane life which hurts him to the quick.
He wants the comfort of distance where love
Will not lean against the crest of his anger,
Solid as silence.

And oh I am tempted to be the woman who holds
The cure—the mother-child-lover who divines
The storm's inner eye of honesty where he waits
Like a newborn on its first morning of knowing,
Where he is the boy who never fails at any test,
Who holds the keys to doors he will not use,
Who says he cannot see the pain his madness
Leaves on a landscape where love lies
Shrouded under the moon's dimming light.

The Year I Found Myself Under
Two Blue Moons

I like jam but not flim-flam
Com'on, baby, knock me a kiss
—LOUIS JORDAN

Here is what the moon advised after clocks
Stopped keeping regular time and I stopped
Following lust like some checkered flag
Behind any old strong profile "Face up"
The moon said under a pluperfect
Time warp of *I had\had not*—past implied

That mad moon knocked me back to first
Date days when I waited by silent telephones
For who-knows-what fool's call and everyone

I fucked was a mystery Might well have spent
The rest of my time fucking my life away
If it weren't for those who told
Me who to fuck and when to fuck and where
Until I said Fuck it and followed the life
Of a poet falling under the spell of dreamlight

Now blowing out sixty and still able
To shake my tambourine to the tune
Ohh, you sexy thing . . . (don't let them tell
    you different: good black don't
    crack and age ain't a number—
    it's articulation of the spine)
Com'on Baby, I've still got coins

Left in this bag unspent But might have thrown
Good money after bad when the Personals took
My fancy Fell in with a magician—some old

Flim-flam man so full of tricks I grew nervous
Watching the waiter trying to fill a water glass
Sure enough the stuff turned blue then red
"For your passion" Mr. Magic said and I knew
Everything I knew was up for grabs
Including cards he said would tell all and

I called for the check and moved on—found
Myself seduced by a man who told me I shouldn't
Be afraid to let my flower bloom again

Wouldn't listen when I explained how
Some odd forty years ago in an act committed
By prescription—my own—I had lost
My only flower to a neighbor's older brother
Can't remember his name But later there was one
Who reminded me of lovers who took women after
Me with glow-in-the-dark bodies

All the while trying to forget what it was
To hold sweet velvet curves and fall
Dappled in sequins of the moon's ghost light

In my life I've loved even those given names
More accurate than their own: Mr. Spark
Mr. No-chin and Ol' Mr. Turtle sweaters
To hide his wrinkled neck and fingers too thick
To hold a tea cup (in vain I hoped
The rest of him would be as interesting)

Then there was the private detective:
The gumshoe the shamus (couldn't resist
Having my own Private Dick) In the end

I failed to make a case for surveillance
Duck and run and even Mr. Wonderful began
To look better if I could keep him in focus
Long enough to make him real (found myself
Dreaming of the magician how smoothly
He pulled coins from my ear or told the future

In the shape of a tear) When Mr. Wonderful
Disappeared (or I imagined him gone)
I began to see in water clear as moonlight

How I was moving into a new century
Hormones no fucking wiser than before
And I left it at that in this dream year
Of two blue moons and triple nines
Practicing perfect zeroes
O like lips ready to be kissed

The Vixen Speaks to the Last Full Moon
of the Century

Moon I've had it with you
Triffling light hungry for corners.
Moon hanging so low bright shadows

Dodge cobwebs & mouse tracks
Lidless eye so moon wide I swear
I see my own reflection.

What have you given me moon?
Decades of hopeful nights
Some cryptic notes written

In footprints dancing
On leafshadows between houses
Or lacing backseats of Chevrolets?

Listen: what I need is back-
Ground music a sleazy lounge
Combo playing old bluesy tunes:

>   *a trip to the moon on gossamer wings*
>   *by the light of the silvery moon*
>   *I want to spoon*

A bagatelle of lousy ballads
Something untranslatable a witch's
Moon or a ballroom chandelier

All expiring on the passport
Of my pitiful imagination—
But what I get is stone sober

You astonishing my house of empty
Rooms lunarfull brightest starshine
Of more than a century—could you

Tonight perhaps be kind as once
Again I dance alone in you-know-what
Light? You can't say I haven't been

Faithful—remember high school when I
Looked at the Rorschach & saw
Exactly what I wasn't supposed to see:

No man-in-the-moon but two cannibals
Dancing around a pot—genitals etched
In silver light—remember the sweet boy

You sent that young Renard who turned
Tail and fled slapping the little dog
Snapping at his heels—running headlong

To bay alone in your midnight glow?
Not much has changed—my memory
Still fills with bad moon lyrics

I mourn still the last silver fox
Gone to some place where even hounds
Will not follow. For 3 months he rode

Me hard to hell in a handbasket
Yet if any night he'd call—bedazzled
By your light—I wait at the garden gate

And wax or wane risk being moonstruck.
Tonight my horoscope warns: the moon
Rises full to kiss the earth & sure

Enough there you are overblown and low
To the ground as if left unsaddled
By restless stars & damned if I'm not over
The moon: in love with cow spoon and all.

PART III

And they danced by the light of the moon . . .

Some Are Dead and Some Are Living

1. Senesta

St. Louis evenings spoiling under electric lights
We leaned out the window above the tavern roof.
Her name better than any song on the juke box.
I'd say: Senesta, Look! That one and That.
The sights male and musk: new smells inside some
Teenage fantasy and no one more surprised
Than us when the answer—deep as Wardell's
Cool bass jazz—floated up through the window
And grabbed us by the scruff.
Left us feeling bad as any tough girl
Worse even—knowing we could never be.
And the lights flickering *Bud Bud Budweiser*
And the night inching toward dawn
And the two of us hanging forever over the sill.

2. Kay Frances

Led that prairie town around by the nose she did
As if her tar paper house wasn't built right
On Kansas tracks and kinky hair wasn't a dead give-away
Even with light skin, grey eyes and all.
She was townie queen and I rose to her summons, floating
With the others from college across double iron rails.
Left me singing: *Don't the moon look lonesome*
When passing trains rattled the wallpaper pattern.
And I pretended not to hear the Great Northern
Or Eastern Flyer shaking coffee cups filled with gin

While bidwhist plays danced on the Naugahyde table.
Ice cubes slammed against my teeth like home runs
And mulatto-boned Kay behind a sweet curtsey smile
Watched me play, shivering in the tunnel of sounds.

3. Margaret

No doubt we always thought of leaving
That town reeking of beef on the hoof
The heel and toe of rundown cowboy boots
12th and Vine littered in bad blues.
We said we had plans to cross more lines
Than the packing house bridge separating states.
We wanted to make it big in some place
Where colors meant more than they appeared
And prairies were no more permanent than celluloid.
Now I hear pregnant with baby boys you turned
Almost religious—could have sworn—nearly did
After I skipped town singing: *Rocky Raccoon.*
I held your voice miles away and that last
Phone call so far so close to my ear.

4. Snow

Behind your back we said it was your attitude
But something more elusive made us marvel
At the stance you took, feet toed out and ready
With the part of you that was hoodlum trapped
In a crazy mix of caprice and avarice.
If there had been tracks down the middle
Of this town, I would have met you crossing
And no matter what, asked whether
I was going the wrong way—Let me guess
You never needed anyone to tell you
It's tough out here and nobody dared
Call you half-pint even with that gravelly

Voice and nail hard way you don't touch, your skin
Velvet shadows as we reach and you turn away.

5. Toni Cade

Even when I tell you Seattle rolls up
At midnight you won't take no for an answer.
Hell, you couldn't take no for a question.
So we drive miles for the sake of Ethiopian
Cowpeas, kifto and spongy bread served
Under fading posters of drylongso countries.
By word of mouth we stay alive, you say
Out here, you say, justice wears a newspaper hat
A single word in print dissolves whole families.
Over your shoulder, sidama stones rise from a poster.
We talk about moods and shrugs and why paths cross.
It's the stories, you say, the stories and I watch
You wet your finger in a bowl of rough salt
Lick it clean and say: sometimes even this is sweet.

6. Jennie

Perhaps in your half-sleep world
You are still dancing in the living room
Rug thrown back to the quick kiss
Of your feet on bare wood floors.
Perhaps each visit merely interrupts
A day you remember best wordless
Behind the slow flutter of eyelids.
Perhaps you still guide us half-grown
Girls through hours of etiquette on how
To pour the proper rise of champagne
In water glasses or how right to find
Four leaves on clover growing in gutters.
Perhaps sweet Auntie the moon you taught me
To dream is still lovely and you remember to believe.

7. Fingerprints

Marked by a time when there were sidewalk games
And boundaries of the heart and home, we broke
Rules: *don't cross the tracks, step on the cracks.*
What our mothers didn't know didn't hurt them.
We grew like Topsy into women, no roads to pave
Our way, no looking back. I'd like to say we never
Attended to skin color, slapping palms for Mary Mack
Pick-up sticks and Jacks. I'd like to say I recall
Your faces clear as the day I tore my seersucker dress
Climbing a fence or took my first kiss under a night
Sky full of fireflies. I need to tell you this:
How memory served up in bits and pieces and yesterdays
Becomes so déjà-vu, I swear I almost see all of you
Standing there in the corner of the room.

Duty

I know now I'm here
more than half a century later
because Fanny died
of a botched abortion
and Papa wasn't about to lose
another daughter to the butcher's knife.
Or maybe it was Jessie
slumping over the dining table
blood oozing onto the carpet
and what Papa saw in her eyes
sealing forever my fate.
And now you call baiting me
with duty saying I should
be there to take care
of your mistake to be the ultimate
daughter cleansing all your wounds
to take care to take care
to suffer the sentence
some man long ago
passed on both of us
in the name of love.

Electra

ya'll come by and see me
I'm as good as it gets
—BAG LADY'S REFRAIN

a woman the daughter said shedding
her clothing shoes coat skirt
one piece then another in front
of the fountain I sat on the bus
headphones in place the woman
was speaking what I could not hear

perhaps said the mother she remembers
her own mother appearing in public
naked or nearly the music deliberate
a '60s protest of what too often we
hide under some slender guise of youth
a fever stolen from the moon's 7th house

a woman she said in front
of the fountain nearly naked I saw
her almost your complexion and old
by the looks of belly skin sagging
with years but I could not hear her with the bus
too crowded and the last stop already passing

how could you not see her wave
the flag of liberation her clothing
shed under a clear autumn sky ashy husk
of skin exposed to the business of the day
going by brisk and unfeeling hoping perhaps
someone her daughter would notice at last

if either could see then the Wedding-of-Rivers
and who rode the main float at Veiled Prophet's
Ball and where were the founders of cities
that burned then the children who wept
and the women left crying for fathers
and brothers on what moon-struck night

a woman I saw bared her breasts in public
a disgrace to God though no one could watch
who knows when these people are hurting
or crazy besides I was listening to music
of churches while everyone waited and prayed I
would see her would help her because she was black

perhaps then she saw her own mother's reflection
alone and single lighting a candle when all
seemed despair Oh Mother Oh Mary please help
my poor children help me walk one more
job to another my body hurting for someone
to hold me I beg you please Mary Amen

she said maybe I wondered if I should have
helped her a woman wild with so many words
but you never know if those people are crazy
and God's music closing out pagans had gathered
so close in my ears then the bus turned
the corner and all my thoughts followed

if the daughter could see what the mother
could remember should someone dare ask her
to roll back the years the war barely over
the men coming home one woman left standing
hip deep in the ruins another left dancing in muddy
water one left hanging from the edge of a bridge

come back to me said mother to daughter
we'll shed skin together burnt amber becoming
one unto the other we'll speak together
or else hardly ever ears opened or plugged
we'll take time to notice the world
sliding past us with no stops between

Bad Slam Broadway

(for Gwendolyn Brooks)

Saturday nites we come cellophaned
in outrageous rags hair dyed
day-glo Martian and body pierced

and we come into 2.4 canned
luke warm beer to drums syncopated
under heavy 5 string electrified

acoustic keys dance body-slammed
filling the floor holler hip-hopped
BREAK IT DOWN arms and legs gyrated

pounding to a broken beat heard
in half-notes and lip-synched
cheap CDs someone napstered

off somebody's downloaded
collection something swiped
off a bad cut called Funked

we cool we bitched out razzed
some 21st century punk rocked
out in one fell swoop remixed

until bloody melody dis-in-tergrated
somewhere near dawn some Starbucked
sunrise we come near collapsed

Teaching G.I.s to Dance

first you lay down
the rules knowing this
war or the next
will take one of them
and you may be the last
girl they hold
so you lay down
the moves the quick-step
samba the three prong
tango the detente that keeps
partners on their feet

you say: don't
wear your combat boots
keep your hands off
my butt don't
move your lips
when you count the steps
and you hope the basics
stick hand-in-hand
that one-two-three-hutt
of any dance

you slip past
the cut-out feet
glued to the floor
this war or the next
and the feet can slide
of their own accord
remember the beat

remember the hips
move first remember
what follows and how
fast you stumble

you run out of time
to prove your point
the one dance they
might learn the one
that might save them
and all you can teach
them is to watch where
their feet take them
and you want to hold
them back to have them
waltz forever in a ball-
room full of meaningless
music and peace

What I Wish for when I Bother
to Wish at All

(for Lou Oma)

one day we will sit on your patio and drink apple martinis forever and
the kid next door will forever throw airplane parts on the roof while leaves
brush the cracked bricks and a stray cat wanders through thin strains of
CD music pitched at odd angles to light we'll flirt with beauty and win its
fickle heart and when asked we'll say: no not us we weren't doing anything
there's nothing to do but we'll speak of being the last daughters of daughters
of sadness and how tears will cleanse the eyes and before all is said and
done we'll recall a time when falling in love was too easy and every night
seemed like the very best night ever and then we'll reinvent the heart we'll
speak of loves lost as if regret arrived smiling with flowers and we'll praise
favorite poems and songs devoted to memory and we'll praise the silenced
poets we'll watch the young walk toward morning the day so close the
moon barely gives way to the sun

Photolinen: La Push Beach

ignore the tides and waves
dropping you against a sheer cliff
here the sea makes the rules

you have to climb the headlands
stumble cross numerous hidden streams
enter a cocoon of fog or follow animal

tracks through moss and sand
find solitude in a whale's jaw bone
or a kind of bird you've never before seen

above sea stacks geese ribbon
toward the horizon of a curdled sky
eagles hit updrafts and glide

on twenty foot waves of air like surfers
gulls fake the maneuvers
where sky hunkers behind thick clouds

streaked like children's fingerprints
whales hump in perfect arcs
sound and spume five perfect spouts

we two imperfect once called each other lovers
now we barely move in the sludge of aftermath
while you clamber along rocks

surefooted and bound for adventure
I sit, feet planted firmly on sand
streaking my legs clean up to scars

marking every ocean I've encountered
from Indian to the Aegean and my ankles
pulse with the various tides

Heartache: Things to Watch for

(for Marisis)

damn weather that keeps getting in the way too hot or too cold the wind
carrying dust motes that lodge in the left corner of your eye horizon blurred
under a low ceiling of clouds everything spongy all day rain we walk like
sailors on a ship atilt in stormy waters   we laugh at leaves turned wrong
side up like eyelids we dance the palm tree dance of hulas watch lightning
nailing derricks to loading docks mountain ridges lit like Xmas and where
transformers explode the sky turned luminous blue from light falling too
far from heaven   sky lit like a single match head or the luminaire of
bombs: blue/green   blue/green as if some x-ray shot the whole hillside
dark to light   it's not enough not with your heart sledge hammer heavy
and rain too gentle to be a threat not when your tongue holds the smell of
the sea or a lost kiss wind howling like the wail of blues songs at ground
level we learn to believe every note every echo of storms thunder sweep of
a big broom and lovers wandering wet and hungry beside the mystery of
the sea beckoned by the moon's first light

Blues for the Slimes House

you reek of chewing garlic
it seeps into your blood
along with the arsenic oozing

out of the smelter's molten
slop of gold silver and platinum
cooking in a room that grows
muscular with heat days you don't

work the house you ride the fork
lift your mind dancing on a four-wheel-
drift about a million miles away

knowing death takes your kind
mid-fifties on the average but now
you sweat pheromones and blood
make wisecracks through aching teeth

it's slag work slopping
around inside tanks ten feet deep
in copper slime and hoping

overtime makes up for the loss
of breath and patience with the old lady
and how your belly aches when you come
and the union takes a cut of your last nerve

you say: *If we had the guts we'd bust*
loose this crap and highjack our way
into a fortune of gold-filled sludge

some days you're a dancing wiseass
trying to overturn Dante's hometown
while the fire does its own demon dance
and the furnaceman cores the clay

until it spills a copper river into the ladle
the black smelterman's down there in his shoulder-
sling of leather commanding fire like an old-world

gladiator and you sit easy atop the crane
cigar in place below yellow porkpie
like you haven't read the union-busters' signs
telling workers: *THROW THE COMMIE IN THE FIRE*

ride easy baby cause tomorrow they shift you back
to the slimes house where fumes
sear your lungs but you can't die now

cause shit you haven't met me yet
and Tacoma's gonna close the damn plant
in a few years anyway leaving you
and a hundred or so smeltermen

trying to remember air without the foul
breath of copper molds and arsenic fumes
a world where death comes if you lose the beat

between fire and rod molten slag and home or how
you stroke that gear stick like it was your woman
a world where all you can do is snort and smoke
and wish for a little loving where we lay

body to body and oh baby
a world made for the wanting of it all

Light Reflecting Glass in the Evelyn Room

The eye sees no form . . .
From light, shades and color
we construct the visible world
    —GOETHE

in this room shadows still remember
how boats were born from colors and shades
of wood when seamen navigated the stars—
now glass blowers mimic sailors their light
falling on an old ship's name held to the wall
in weathered letters : *Evelyn*

and the glassmaker's fire holds constellations
of stars while the blowers spend
their days reading the gel of colors
trapped in pockets of earth the way sailors
once read passage in the light of skies

their legs seek even keels as they straddle
benches and ride the language of lip and tongue

against flames they waltz to the heat
of their own pulse coax silica
to claim its shape while they spin
steaming wands of liquid glass—
the same way tall tales spin out of any
sailor's passion in some foreign port

inside the fire's vortex light is a whoosh
that holds only when kieselguhrs melt in colors
spindled hot by a blower's kiss—
and they are cavaliers who know to keep casual
as a handshake or vagrant sex

the touch of lips and tongue dancing
against heat they know they must be quick

and the trick of the kiss is the beauty
of lingering just long enough
for the egg of clay to expand like lungs—
long enough for sintering light
to turn muted in reflected heat

the orb of earth clings to the blowpipe
in colors more liquid than solid : gold
into red black to amber and white
like tides shifting too quickly to shore

wind mimics the harmony of breath and fire
as they bend to their work
tender as lovers or just as impatient—
they know a shape is something to catch in transit:
light turned to shadow colors changing in fire

a memory like love visible only to their eyes
they look for perfection dropping errant shapes

to the floor and the mercy of inconstant light
where moved too quickly from the heat of their kiss
cast-off forms explode of their own accord—
a spontaneous combustion like bad marriages
or those human torches featured in the *Enquirer*

or like stars gone nova exploding under the sky
sailors used to set time by—
the same sky destined for the ghost ship : *Evelyn*
now lost to all but the blower's oven—
barnacles still salted in its vowels

just as the wind traps in wood the shape
of oceans what is held in diatomaceous earth waits
for the sweet breath of a blower's kiss to soar
into colors of startled suns : or else breaks
apart like hearts under sudden conflict of heat

a breath bonded in a uvula of flames the blower's
fire spelling out shapes with its selfish mouth

Telling Lies

(for KLJ)

He took the first in his youth when he thought he'd never find a mate He took the second because the water she served one night in a truck stop was crystal clear her apron crisp as fresh toast   The third came out of fear of loving the first too much   The fourth was a fluke but the fifth was nearly his undoing when he found she collected husbands like bright buttons preserving names in unlabeled pickling jars   The sixth was too young and reminded him of his mother who had used the moon as a mirror   The seventh was of a different race and age just to be on the safe side   The eighth would have worked until he realized she was too much like the fifth with her tinkling laugh and bad habit of calling him by another name :: Oh *that* husband she exclaimed :: And only when he reached a baker's dozen did he discover what they had been cooking up how they ran together in the sex of it all in smells and lips those little quirks carried to bed   And that day when the moon persisted in staying in a sun swollen sky they gathered on his doorstep   Each with a fish grinning its last grin hook still baited   Each with a brand new ten-speed built for the roughest roads   Only when they had stitched him up   Only then when it was too late to turn back did he have any second thoughts

Reckless Divas

one day she looked
in the mirror and saw
her own mother
wrinkles set
like bobby-pin curls
what are you looking for
the mirror asked
    have you darned
    all the socks my dear
    stacked the good
    will boxes full
    of size sixes
    you'll never wear
for days after she never
even glanced at the mirror
afraid of what she might
see or moreover not see
that girl who smiled
back at her so arrogantly
that once she nearly lost
herself in the dreamy
reflection of it all
    with the mirror half
    covered she asked
oh girl, if you leave
me now I'll forget how
to hip swing
pick up the pace
    waltz samba
    should I lead
    should I follow

without you girl
I am a sodden dish
cloth an unhemmed
skirt of wrinkled silk
the mirror gave off a strange light
act your age, act your age
the mirror glared but she answered
there's so much left
to be done and undone
 promises to be kept
 loves to unravel
 a bulky trashbag
 of memoirs
 turned to mush
my heart left in a mess
while some fool's out there
retelling all my secrets
on color TV selling
over the counter remedies
 ask me now
 ask me now
 ask me now
 for a limited time
finally the day came when
without asking she shied
away from the mirror and joined
the illustrious ladies of Former
Head-turners Anonymous
high-toned women dancing
in sunlight shining
through a veil of leaves
and whatever else loiters
in attics thick with old
rpm platters cds shiny
as flying saucers and the rain
forever drumming the same tune

more to remember
less to forget
more to remember
less to regret
and oh the ladies put on
perfect faces and executed
a bossa nova half turn
then shimmied out of sight
stepping fast into the long day
clocks ticked wildly
and the mirror danced
with a young girl
who laughed
at all its jokes

Travelling Moon

the pilot swoops
low over the North
Pole—new lakes
have formed

once again
you are leaving
a lover or returning

you try to remember
if you've doused the fire
under the coffee or turned

off all the lights
you wonder if the land below
holds a house you remember

and look:
that shadow limb
where the moon shatters
on the knuckle of sky

Ballad for the Blue Moon Tavern

Saturday nights when the tavern
really rocked, the girl perched
on the slice of neon moon above

the door winked while poets
gathered, their bar stools notched
like some gunslinger's belt—

certain seats reserved for hotshots
who crowded in before the fake moon
glowed full blue against

the cobalt blue of the northern night
sky:: and just for the record, the pin-up
girl kept count of who walked in

and where they sat—Dylan Thomas
there and Carolyn and David huddled
in that corner and over there

Dick Hugo—who years later sober
claimed he couldn't understand
what folks did with all that time

on their hands—but those nights
in the Blue Moon no one mentioned
time and how Dylan's days were numbered

or how long before John Logan morose
as ever stumbled home to his houseboat
where the lake spread its tawdry skirt

welcoming any moon—those nights time
was measured on Picard's barometric light
    while the Blue Moon mocked the real moon

    cresting above the tips of regal pines—
and the pin-up girl nested in the arc of moon
    above the door asked in the spit and hiss

    of tubing which one cast the best
light and which held the most stars
    in its sway:: on those nights

    the sky was arctic blue and the land
truly emerald and the town
    before it moved upscale was still

    in love with itself and all of us above
all else in love with that lunar light

PART IV

The owl looked up to the moon above
sang to a sweet guitar . . .

Mae West Chats It Up with Bessie Smith

You hadn't oughta kiss a girl if you're carrying a gun.
—RAYMOND CHANDLER

once I found a cowboy   who thought he could
ride me into the New   West and God
put rollers on the bed   to make his journey smoother
last time I saw him   he looked the worse for wear
hair all but gone   gut eating his belt
he was a sight   all laid out in a new suit
(same one I bought him)

honey he had a Corvette and the morals
of a chinchilla   but just enough
gangster to satisfy my   Kansas City longings
oh he was handsome   as you know the devil was
in his eyes and his clothes   slick as sharkskin
some kinda silk worn close   and groin sweet
like morning rain   inside a buttercup

cept he dropped his pants and showed me
something for the cat to play with

thought he'd stopped me on the road
he did but when I said come up and see me
I was already heading in another direction

then there was that business   with some woman
he wouldn't name   now would naming matter sugah
you gotta know who you're aiming for   just aim
or the light   of one cigarette to the next
always someone there with a match   and an itch
to scratch   what hurts long as your voice holds

What Happened to the Rabbit

Ask Alice she'll talk
about searching for an idealist's
dream how falling
through the hole she'd expected
a change for the better a chance
for the good guys to win

But it's the beginning of the century
or the end the rabbit gripes
everybody's rich—Alice fumbles
with the carrot hanging from her stick

Is there anything as clear
as what's homegrown she asks
the rabbit squeezes out one
more tear Royalty he says
is dead or is it democracy
I forget—Alice frets

The Tweedle brothers raise interest rates
think corporate the rabbit insists
to think to sleep perchance to think
again he grins—What on earth happened

Alice asks—once when I was taller I moved
in a circle of friends who wanted
to live and learn now I'm older
and those chickens are home to roost
everyone wants only to earn and earn
The hole isn't big enough

for individual pranks the rabbit sighs
Now look at the mess you've made
someone has to scrub the stairs and buff
the windows clean—think like a man

Alice nods—are these your glasses
the rabbit asks rose tinted lenses
glinting brilliantly as diamonds
I've forgotten the words Alice says
one for all alas alack a name that ends
in an X—or a Y the rabbit interrupts

Oh love the road is long and I can't go
home throw me the bone of lost years
Get real the rabbit grunts
and thumps away down the dark

The Moon in the Dragon's Mouth

Once upon a time the moon moved in any direction it wished—not just east to west but north to south and north by northeast or south and reverse—one night the dragon saw it shining so bright in the sky she was stopped in her tracks, frozen like a moth—in candlelight like a woman rising naked and scented from her bath (for it is well known that winged dragons are female and remain so until the urge to mother overcomes them and they lose their wings—a most dangerous woman, one left to her own wiles)—the moon was not impressed by questions of gender, caught as it were in how to stay afloat and what direction to take—the dragon saw the moon moving and thought: this is what I want, this gem in the sky, so perfect a pearl: luminescent pale fire—the moon thought nothing, amused by what was mistaken for mountains, craters, the ratio of light reflected on earth—the moon paid no heed to its own power and scattered its pale blue light in every nook and cranny—seers and soothsayers cried: moon madness moonstruck lunacy beware but the dragon flicked her tail and bellowed a greeting—the moon rode on—devil moon the seers whispered—the dragon reared on her hind legs and reached but the moon saw its own shadow and with a blink of the sun it was gone, the dragon left thrashing air behind it: trickster light firestone moonstone—and the soothsayers huddled to question who had stolen the moon: a dog someone said, a rabbit, a man, a wolf—and no one saw the dragon until the moon had all but vanished in the halo of sun until the dragon lifted herself once more and grabbed the moon between her teeth—but the sun had warmed the moon and what was ice was fire and what was fire was cold more wine than water more opal than pearl—October light amber moon yellow moon blood orange—and moonstruck the dragon twisted her head this way and that: left to right left to right—the moon had no choice but to follow suit: east to west east to west, no more to wander where ever—a perfect wedding of ice and fire dragon and moon—some nights you still see the hot breath of the dragon circling the moon—rain tomorrow the soothsayers whisper—some nights when the dragon turns, all you can see is a slice of moon a quarter moon a half and some nights the dragon flicks her tail and her wings clap together like thunder

Wonder Woman

finally you're tired of playing
Wonder Woman—that invisible
plane becoming more nuisance
than blessing—fly too low

and you risk ground fire
too high and weather socks you in
there's always something
you invent yourself again

and again as if the lightning
bolt on your breast isn't enough
and the docs asking how long as if
you could remember when

that streak of heaven's fire
appeared—so wrapped up
as you were in surviving the day
to day routine of what passed

for small talk around the water
cooler and who had won the latest
prize or yet another great review
and how years never stick to you

the mystery is that you kept
it going for so long
the plane the golden lasso
and lightning bolt—ignoring

the nagging feeling that it all
all depends on smoke and mirrors
living only for the lift off
the sudden rush of leaving earth behind

Fairy Tales

Some daughters were bred to be
caretakers, obedient simply
for the sake of obedience

Some daughters grow fat
with worry and call that love
Some were born for beauty

Some were sturdy, born for work
and breeding daughters like themselves
Some daughters soften like well

tanned hides—some cut their teeth
doing what not to do so well
they can't be called anyone's daughter

Some hold love in their baskets
of goodies—some tsk-tsk sew up
their mouths until nothing escapes

Some daughters work all day
at being good daughters
Some only howl at the moon

for nights on end, forever
the stepchild, the other woman
standing in the backdoor

the princess who says: fuck
the pea and throws the damn
mattress out the window

The Princess

She did everything
according to royal
demands—let down
her hair, tried on
all the kingdom's shoes
counted the dwarves
from one to seven every
night, helped the maids
hang out the clothes
despite blackbirds flocking
to watch, cameras under
their wings—all this
she did in less than
seven years times seven
in less than a twinkle
or repeating Rumple-
stilskein a hundred times
under the full moon
all this and nothing
could save her trapped
as she was in that awful
frigid family with its
cauldron of secrets
and despite the carriages
of Lord Chancellors
and the trail of paparazzi
nothing could save her
from the cold prophecy
of never belonging

Unlearning the Brothers Grimm

Frau Viehmann's *marchen* became timeless tales of discovery.
—DIE BRÜDER GRIMM

in the end the girl
   did not remember sagging
      tenements/gangways lacing

old bricks like loose chains
   in the end the girl
      remembered her grandmother's

stories of faraway castles
   and a prince and for all
      of her wishing no color

of skin/ hair bunched like buttons
   or dreaded sheep's wool/ eyes round
      as the moon tucked behind them

       * * *

so she fashioned herself
from Aida and Sheba
she practiced their kisses
their smiles and their charms
those stories that fit her
those grand happy endings
the moon in her fifth house
the night in her arms

       * * *

the stories they closed the gap
   between telling and the stink
      of the kitchen/the hog belly sausage

and pale chicken feet/the dumplings
   all seasoned with blackberries stolen
      the girl dreamed in forests so dark and

so deep where witches might lurk/or worst
   if she dared think of men
      from the pool halls and barber

shops/taverns, the vagrants and junkies
   of street corner/alleys, the smoke curls
      and shadows from Frau Viehmann's woods

      * * *

Hey little black girl walking down the street
Hey little black girl looking mighty sweet

      * * *

Once in the trash bin she found a tiara
and thinking it discarded perhaps in the haste

of fumbling home, plucked it soiled
from the rotting heap and doctors said she might

lose fingers infected as they were
with the disease of fondling

      * * *

Last night the night before twenty-
four robbers at my door :: ALL HID!

      * * *

But stories they taught her
as surely as prayer books
that around the next corner
or the end of the road
the prince would be waiting

in some mist covered valley
if only she'd wander a map
in one hand her heart in the other

      * * *

  how she moved in this impossible dance
    herself imagined in each of the tales
      closing the gap between telling and self
        until all that was real was unreal

      * * *

and not even when the prince fell
upon her like a log

(what luck he thought when he caught her
sleeping—and creased his pants so and none

would be the wiser) never did she see
the day when she'd lose the power to choose

which way the wind blows—when no longer
was she beautiful so full of candy kisses

and self-lubricating favors—when the flick
of wrists mahogany brown as tree trunks was not

enough to catch the blush of any would-be
lover—never imagined the days disappearing

when even a frog would do if he could carry a tune
(though only a few understood

she preferred serenading violins and tenor sax
over Baby-dowah-what-you-do-do-do)—she was down

to brass tacks to cold hard facts to what
was available given some invisible "use by" date

      * * *

then the bittersweet reminder of what
had slipped past her when she was sassy
and fast when the magic of hips round
as plums/ of legs lean and long could make
men sing Blues they'd never heard of
(Honey with those legs that smile
she once commanded the birds to sing)

      * * *

finally she began eyeballing the losers::
the luckless first son who had more than once

mistaken himself for the scullery
maid and lost his lips in a mirror

or the overgrown boy who kept his crown
in a hatbox for wont of a miller who worked

silver—even the old one whose beard
turned grey with each fart:: nothing a potion

wouldn't fix she thought—a little seasoning
in the pot—a little salt to make it right

happily-ever-after kiss kiss kisses
and flowers gracing her crépè-paper hair

      * * *

> *Once upon a time the goose*
> *drank the wine the monkey*
> *played the fiddle on the street*
> *car line   the street car broke*
> *the monkey got choked*
> *and all went to heaven*
> *but the sanctified folk*

      * * *

oh for the time when the world was all
story books and she was the princess
of the front stoop—a time when only
she could weave happy endings—not here
with the smell of all her dreams
burning—not here where no castles
were hers to keep
     how eager might we all be to live where
       time stops inside a tale told and retold

          * * *

  no matter how fast or slow
     she ran/ no matter how many
        awards she dragged behind
        she was no closer than before

          * * *

nowadays a girl's got to do what a girl's got to
so she tossed her book with its vague markings

of castles and its doodle rings of crowns
and she wandered down the road where the mist

beckoned (there is always mist in such stories)
where time waited patient as an ox and the only

holes she feared falling into were easily repaired
where her footprints left impressions so small

they could be mistaken for silk dropped
from a spinning wheel and where when she rested

she caught a glimpse of the moon drifting
like a stray balloon toward the edge
of the known world into another story

     ready to unfold:: and shoes in hand
       she danced alone under a starburst sky

Eartha Takes the Old Woman
Shopping for Red Shoes

because neighbors
don't speak
and never stay put

because the weather
dies slowly in scenic
skies because

for once the heat
stays longer than geese
because you let too many

moons change
your mind
and buying

red shoes means
exceptional days
when clocks

run uphill and back
to better days
when red

oh bloody youth
all fire and brass
when red

lasted whole nights
after you've seen
too many sunsets

where laughter spools
into primary colors
days all smudge-proof

full of crisp
seasons and moons
waxing full

and Eartha whispers
over your shoulder
if somebody asks

just take them
back to '53
or '68 if pushed

when rock and roll
was the real thing
and we were slick

as kittens and purred
long black legs ending
in patent red shoes

Song of the Red Kimono

(for Alice Fulton)

in the red kimono the woman
who spoke becomes the woman
spoken about : impervious in red

the woman flowered and unveiled
defines the colors of sunsets==
the red kimono reminds her

of poems she has written
and poems forgotten while she
stood on balconies at dawn

while deserts bloomed
and mountains rose out of mists==
for fifty years they covered

the world in countries A to Z
excluding X and paths she tries
not to forget : the woman who wrote

becomes the woman written about
in red becomes Nefertiti stepping
lightly onto Nubia's shores

remembering evenings in Tangiers
and Tibet the lost cities of Peru
the moon nested above the ruins

of Karnak or kissing pink marble
temples at Petra : in the red kimono
she is foreign at home everywhere==

each pocket balances keys
the silk shedding wrinkles
in each city for the woman

indescribable draped from neck
to hem in a color assuredly
outrageous : a poet's gift

to a poet greeting her each night
in hotel rooms of distance where
mornings begin with indecipherable

maps : and the kimono circles
and settles from shoulders to hips
in whispers of red against black==

after shower bath and oils
after poems emerge from its folds
silk crooning to its own mystery

Last Dance for the Copper Room
Hot Springs Band

it's cha-cha and waltz time and grey-haired
sambas and folks called seniors gliding

under an artificial moon of reflected glass spinning
silent above twenty by thirty parquet squares

it's the last resort on a mirror lake where waters
move sluggish as arthritic bones and all

the fish died years ago when the plant
flushed sewage off-shore it's the route

vaudevillians took when the trail was still
a moon dance of light carved in pristine woods

it's the old folks home and memories of summer
crowds in tight skin and thin bathing suits

it's the silence of the spa's mist-soaked shade
raccoons gliding by in stadium coats dragging

stones washed in the earth's sulfur tongue
it's the town's one steady neon sign boasting

SWIMMING*POOL*DANCING and musicians so old
they play tunes just to recreate themselves

it's the six or eight banded geese flocked
to a place where dozens once fouled the water

and nearly shut out the sun on their return
each spring it's the echo of a call to arms

where Indians were chased for the hunt and winds
sang the deaths of Copper Creek or Mallard Point

it's the place where no racists are registered
and the town claims it's clean behind locked gates

it's the one-two step of folks who look
as if they've ironed out all their mistakes

it's the better life they've worked for
the corporate beat that's going to keep them

where at last they have nothing
else to do but face the music and dance

Vienna Layover

(for Lois B.)

the trick is knowing this geography
won't match any movie or dime-
store novel—stuck in transit
you hope you'll live

to catch a train heading east
on the old Orient Express track—
meanwhile smoke permeates your clothes
pulls your breath

up short like a torn boot strap—
no attorney general's report here
you watch the homeless puff
and cough going nowhere

on the two stone benches facing tracks
going everywhich way—clothes
reek of stale tobacco breath—
America's in litigation

boasting pockets of smokefree counties
but this is old Europe and countries
still owned by Liggett and Myer riding
toward death on cartoon camels

a vast ocean of commerce, all the while
swearing the crossing is harmless—
they sell in any language so your only safe
option is Turkish coffee

ink black sugarless—the Danube rolling
past steeped in bitter wars and sausage
kings—beggars scrounging for loose
change and cork filters—

you check the call board for the next
thing smoking out of town in less
than an hour and while you inhale
a breath someone else spent

too long getting rid of everyone turns
Nosferatu yellow like the bottom of old ash-
trays smoldering in half-smoked butts—
you should have picked

up a carton of cigs, oxygen, and a nurse
along with the *Lonely Planet* guide—
this crowd is rowdy and you're the only
one left waltzing

the lungfish two-step—no breath
for the weary and only the strong
survive—the world here is all tar
and ash and the wheeze

of diesel fumes—the moon sinks
like a stone in the muddy river—
everything on schedule—the station
master calls out numbers

like a croupier—yours garbles into mush—
by this time your train has left—
you search for some place downwind
still flush with the memory of fresh air

Moon Over Turtle Island

August saw pintails drifting
Upcurrent from tour boats
The sunsets even more flambouyant
Under the Aurora bridge where the harbor
Master worries tankers toward Alaska
NOAA flagships edge in their wake. What

Laces the shore dances in shadow
Easy as bald eagles floating on updrafts.
August marks the last month of weather and last
Vestiges of sleepless summer cruises ply the lake
Everywhich way like feathers or pine needles
Something saved for that last postcard home.

We know this is the universe the world
Astride a turtle's back and nothing
Safe in the teeter-totter of water and air
Holding tight for one more ride.

Moon Over Marakesh

in the lobby the ladies
move in sultry light
a splendid act of holding
night at bay under a canopy
of spiced air bells and pipes

listen closely: carriages
pass at easy intervals
below harem windows camels
kneel in a courtyard—
the length of their journey

from the land of the blue
Tuareg is anyone's guess—
here rug merchants stall
for more money sweet tea
a story in trade for time

where desert time bends
rapidly no hour clock—only
the moon the fiction
men live by riding humps
of land for nothing more

than a drink of sweet water
and dreams are no more
than a handful
of dried grass and weeds
brought to souks where bricks

arch narrow streets under signs
written in the fluid curl
and weft of sand strokes—
and all those shades
of black to brown become

the me reflected in copper
pots and silver bangles cast
the old way with flaws made
in hues more beautiful—I fall
in love with the bustle

of mysterious streets and smoke
of sandalwood the kohl ringed
eyes and yards of bright cloth
the place where I am so easily
mistaken for being at home

Loving this Earth

to love ourselves, we must first love the earth . . .
—AFRICAN PROVERB

those I've loved have worn golden hoops
have showered diamonds on a bird's nest
to see the sun catch its own shadow
those I've loved have feasted on loss
the salt of it still fresh on their lips
my loves have danced like drunken sailors
like children high on sugar and afternoons
of freedom—those I've loved have been bold
and brazen, have left home almost grown with little
more than a shoebox of breadcrumbs to trail them
they have been wise and reckless, constant as
an itch before it dulls under the body's armour
they have been beautiful in their bodies
full of secrets of sex, of wild forests and spice
they have been scholars and fiddlers, rebels
and revolutionaries—those I've loved
have been daring as bandits, and Lord yes, poets
who watched the moon and thought it their own
love child, a light on oceans they carelessly mapped
and if I were to do it over again, I would
with more laughter and a confetti of kisses
with the scent of rusted earth, a spray of lavender
the moon at my side, its light in my hair

Notes

Pillow Book:

Peter Greenaway's 1996 film, "The Pillow Book," is an exotic tapestry that unfolds like a story poem with lists of sensual images from the 10th century pillow book or diary of a Japanese noble woman. The film reflects Greenaway's passion for bending time and place. All of the quotes are taken from the movie, except *Everything that happens is to be adored,* which is from James White's essay, "On James Leo Herlihy" (*Seattle Review,* vol. XXII:1, 2000).

I Speak to the Girl Some Dim Boy Loves and *Pillow Book:*

Both are addressed to Richard Hugo and Denise Levertov, respectively, two great teachers who loved the magic of poetic language and rhythms.

Ballad for the Blue Moon Tavern:

The Blue Moon is a landmark tavern in Seattle, Washington, where poets from Dylan Thomas to recent habitues gathered to discuss the politics of verse and the vagaries of the nonliterary world.

The Company She Keeps:

To be caught in the act is couched in the Latin phrase: *in flagrante delicto,* literally, to be discovered while the crime is blazing.

Heartbreak Moon on the Strait of Juan de Fuca:

On calm nights, when the temperature warms the water and the air is still, certain aquatic organisms give off a kind of bluish light called bioluminescence. The reflection is most vivid under the light of a full moon. "Rabbit-in-the-Moon" is the Mayan myth equivalent to "Man-in-the-Moon."

The Year I Found Myself Under Two Blue Moons:

The second full moon of the month is called the proverbial "blue moon." This occurrence commonly takes place only once in any given year. 1999 was unique in that there were two blue moons, in January and March of that year.

The Vixen Speaks to the Last Full Moon of the Century:

The last full moon of the twentieth century, December 22, 1999, winter solstice, was closest to the earth and, subsequently, appeared larger than any moon in the past 133 years.

You and Me and Veronica Lake:

"The man who uses his finger to point to the moon is a wise man. The man who mistakes his finger for the moon is a fool." Chinese proverb.

Light Reflecting Glass in the Evelyn Room:

"Evelyn" is an old shipboard sign hanging in what is now the blowers' room of the Chihuly Glassworks on Lake Union in Seattle.

Blues for the Slimes House:

The slimes house is the smelter room where metals are separated before processing—the hottest and most dangerous room in the smelter.

Bad Slam Broadway:

After Gwendolyn Brooks (1917–2000), "We Real Cool."

Photolinens: LaPush Beach:

Photolinen (or Fotolinen) is a particular type of photographic paper, especially useful to establish mood rather than detail. The paper can be stretched or held flat, depending on the artist's desired subjectivity. Judy Chicago used photolinen to enhance the emotional narrative of images in "The Holocaust Project." Luminos (as in "light" or "moon") is another name for this type of paper.

Moon Over Turtle Island:

Turtle Island was a Native American name for the North American continent.

Telling Lies:

Uses the adage: A woman without a man is like a fish without a bicycle. Quoted from Irina Dunn, and later, Gloria Steinem.

Electra:

Electra of Greek myth was one of the Seven Sisters, a sea nymph whose name means amber. She is the daughter associated with unresolved sexual gratification, often with ambivalent feelings toward the mother and, subsequently, the father's death. In Freudian terms, womb fever and madness are often synonymous. In contemporary Western cultures, homelessness is often thought to be a form of madness. The Veiled Prophet Pageant is held as an annual event in St. Louis, derived from a Mason-Dixon celebration in which the Prophet, dressed in a white conical hat and mask, is paraded through the city on a float beside a beauty queen.

Travelling Moon:

Limb is the thin edge of the moon shadowing the shape of the moon as seen without binoculars.

The Moon in the Dragon's Mouth:

In Chinese mythology, the moon is sometimes depicted as being caught in the open mouth of a dragon riding the rim of the sky. If the dragon's breath is fiery, the moon is red. If the dragon is calm, the moon is yellow. Winged dragons are said to be females.

Unlearning the Brothers Grimm:

The Brothers Grimm transcribed the stories of Frau Viehmann, some of which became *marchen,* or tales that move in an unreal world without definite locale or characters and where heroes succeed to kingdoms and marry princesses. The inner-city chants *Twenty-four robbers* and . . . *the goose drank the wine* are children's games of hide-and-seek and jump rope.

Song of the Red Kimono:

A gift from poet Alice Fulton, in 1982, the red silk kimono has traveled with me around the world, from Tibet to Madagascar. Misdirected to the Seychelles, Cyprus, Austria, and to some unknown corner of the luggage area in Rome for a five-day disappearance, it should have its own frequent flyer miles.

Moon Over Marakesh:

In desert folklore, dreams are defined as a handful of dry grass and weeds.

COLLEEN J. MCELROY is a professor emerita of English and creative writing at the University of Washington in Seattle, Washington. Her publications include two fiction collections, *Jesus and Fat Tuesday* (1987) and *Driving Under the Cardboard Pines* (1990); several volumes of poetry, including *Bones Flames* (1987), *What Madness Brought Me Here—New and Selected Poems 1968–88* (1991), *Queen of the Ebony Isles,* winner of the American Book Award (1984), and *Travelling Music* (1998); and two travel memoirs, *A Long Way From St. Louie* (1997), and most recently, *Over the Lip of the World: Among the Storytellers of Madagascar* (2001).

Illinois Poetry Series

Laurence Lieberman, Editor

History Is Your Own Heartbeat
Michael S. Harper (1971)

The Foreclosure
Richard Emil Braun (1972)

The Scrawny Sonnets and
Other Narratives
Robert Bagg (1973)

The Creation Frame
Phyllis Thompson (1973)

To All Appearances: Poems New
and Selected
Josephine Miles (1974)

The Black Hawk Songs
Michael Borich (1975)

Nightmare Begins Responsibility
Michael S. Harper (1975)

The Wichita Poems
Michael Van Walleghen (1975)

Images of Kin: New and Selected Poems
Michael S. Harper (1977)

Poems of the Two Worlds
Frederick Morgan (1977)

Cumberland Station
Dave Smith (1977)

Tracking
Virginia R. Terris (1977)

Riversongs
Michael Anania (1978)

On Earth as It Is
Dan Masterson (1978)

Coming to Terms
Josephine Miles (1979)

Death Mother and Other Poems
Frederick Morgan (1979)

Goshawk, Antelope
Dave Smith (1979)

Local Men
James Whitehead (1979)

Searching the Drowned Man
Sydney Lea (1980)

With Akhmatova at the Black Gates
Stephen Berg (1981)

Dream Flights
Dave Smith (1981)

More Trouble with the Obvious
Michael Van Walleghen (1981)

The American Book of the Dead
Jim Barnes (1982)

The Floating Candles
Sydney Lea (1982)

Northbook
Frederick Morgan (1982)

Collected Poems, 1930–83
Josephine Miles (1983; reissue, 1999)

The River Painter
Emily Grosholz (1984)

The Ways We Touch
Miller Williams (1997)

The Rooster Mask
Henry Hart (1998)

The Trouble-Making Finch
Len Roberts (1998)

Grazing
Ira Sadoff (1998)

Turn Thanks
Lorna Goodison (1999)

Traveling Light: Collected and
New Poems
David Wagoner (1999)

Some Jazz a While: Collected Poems
Miller Williams (1999)

The Iron City
John Bensko (2000)

Songlines in Michaeltree: New and
Collected Poems
Michael S. Harper (2000)

Pursuit of a Wound
Sydney Lea (2000)

The Pebble: Old and New Poems
Mairi MacInnes (2000)

Chance Ransom
Kevin Stein (2000)

House of Poured-Out Waters
Jane Mead (2001)

The Silent Singer: New and
Selected Poems
Len Roberts (2001)

The Salt Hour
J. P. White (2001)

Guide to the Blue Tongue
Virgil Suárez (2002)

The House of Song
David Wagoner (2002)

X =
Stephen Berg (2002)

Arts of a Cold Sun
G. E. Murray (2003)

Barter
Ira Sadoff (2003)

The Hollow Log Lounge
R. T. Smith (2003)

In the Black Window: New and
Selected Poems
Michael Van Walleghen (2004)

A Deed to the Light
Jeanne Murray Walker (2004)

Controlling the Silver
Lorna Goodison (2005)

Good Morning and Good Night
David Wagoner (2005)

American Ghost Roses
Kevin Stein (2005)

Battles and Lullabies
Richard Michelson (2005)

Visiting Picasso
Jim Barnes (2006)

The Disappearing Trick
Len Roberts (2006)

Sleeping with the Moon
Colleen J. McElroy (2007)

Expectation Days
Sandra McPherson (2007)

National Poetry Series

Other Poetry Volumes

Local Men and Domains
James Whitehead (1987)

Her Soul beneath the Bone: Women's
Poetry on Breast Cancer
Edited by Leatrice Lifshitz (1988)

Days from a Dream Almanac
Dennis Tedlock (1990)

Working Classics: Poems on
Industrial Life
Edited by Peter Oresick and Nicholas Coles
(1990)

Hummers, Knucklers, and Slow Curves:
Contemporary Baseball Poems
Edited by Don Johnson (1991)

The Double Reckoning of Christopher
Columbus
Barbara Helfgott Hyett (1992)

Selected Poems
Jean Garrigue (1992)

New and Selected Poems, 1962–92
Laurence Lieberman (1993)

The Dig and Hotel Fiesta
Lynn Emanuel (1994)

For a Living: The Poetry of Work
Edited by Nicholas Coles and Peter Oresick
(1995)

The Tracks We Leave: Poems on
Endangered Wildlife of North America
Barbara Helfgott Hyett (1996)

Peasants Wake for Fellini's Casanova and
Other Poems
Andrea Zanzotto; edited and translated by
John P. Welle and Ruth Feldman; drawings
by Federico Fellini and Augusto Murer
(1997)

Moon in a Mason Jar and What My
Father Believed
Robert Wrigley (1997)

The Wild Card: Selected Poems,
Early and Late
Karl Shapiro; edited by Stanley Kunitz
and David Ignatow (1998)

Turtle, Swan and Bethlehem in
Broad Daylight
Mark Doty (2000)

Illinois Voices: An Anthology of
Twentieth-Century Poetry
Edited by Kevin Stein and G. E. Murray
(2001)

On a Wing of the Sun
Jim Barnes (3-volume reissue, 2001)

Poems
William Carlos Williams; introduction by
Virginia M. Wright-Peterson (2002)

Creole Echoes: The Francophone Poetry
of Nineteenth-Century Louisiana
Translated by Norman R. Shapiro;
introduction and notes by M. Lynn Weiss
(2003)

Poetry from *Sojourner:*
A Feminist Anthology
Edited by Ruth Lepson with Lynne
Yamaguchi; introduction by Mary
Loeffelholz (2004)

Asian American Poetry:
The Next Generation
Edited by Victoria M. Chang; foreword by
Marilyn Chin (2004)

Papermill: Poems, 1927–35
Joseph Kalar; edited and with an
Introduction by Ted Genoways (2005)

The University of Illinois Press
is a founding member of the
Association of American University Presses.

Composed in 11/14 Adobe Garamond
by Jim Proefrock
at the University of Illinois Press
Designed by Dennis Roberts
Manufactured by Sheridan Books, Inc.

University of Illinois Press
1325 South Oak Street
Champaign, IL 61820-6903
www.press.uillinois.edu